THE LITTLE BOOK OF
ELVIS PRESLEY

Published in 2022 by OH!
An Imprint of Welbeck Non-Fiction Limited,
part of Welbeck Publishing Group.
Based in London and Sydney.
www.welbeckpublishing.com

Compilation text © Welbeck Non-Fiction Limited 2019
Design © Welbeck Non-Fiction Limited 2019

ISBN 978-1-78739-294-6

Compiled and written by: Malcolm Croft
Project manager: Ross Hamilton
Design: Russell Knowles, Luana Gobo
Production: Jess Brisley

A CIP catalogue record for this book is available from the British Library

Printed in Dubai

10 9

Jacket cover photographs: Getty Images

THE LITTLE BOOK OF
ELVIS PRESLEY

INSPIRATIONAL QUOTES FROM
THE KING OF ROCK 'N' ROLL

CONTENTS

INTRODUCTION

Famous for always wanting a little less conversation and a little more action, Elvis Presley let his regal talent – as well as those jigglin' legs – do all the talking. However, despite being a man of so few words – at least with reporters – the King was still as famous for his quick quips and wise wit as any other rock star of his day. Elvis simply chose quality over quantity.

From his earliest Sun recordings in 1954 to his tragic death in 1977, Elvis Presley remained the King of all he surveyed. Like Midas, everything he touched turned to gold – gold discs. That doesn't mean to say it was all good, of course, as the singer-turned-actor admitted repeatedly about several of his 31 (!) movies. But no matter what he put his name to, his legions of loyal fans lapped it up as if it was as delicious as a peanut butter, banana and bacon sandwich.

Elvis Presley quite literally shook up the hearts and minds of 1950s culture with a voice that rippled across America like an earthquake, uniting the States as it did so. Elvis's singing, his songs – his everything – inspired kids all over the world to pick up a guitar, sing into a hairbrush and shake their legs to the beat. With Elvis, music was no longer black and white. It was rock-and-roll music, plain and simple. Today, he remains the only solo artist on earth to sell more than one billion records. Not bad for a poor boy from Memphis, Tennessee, who had to postpone his showbiz career for two years to join the military. Imagine that happening to David Bowie?

In the years since his death, his fans (and countless impersonators) refuse to believe Elvis is gone. Thankfully, with this super-calorific collection of witty quips and wisdom and, of course, his unforgettable music and legacy, Elvis lives on. Hail to the King!

CHAPTER

ONE

LONG LIVE
THE KING

“

Oscar Davis tells me you're sensational. I'm going to see if I can book you on one of my shows.

**Colonel Tom Parker's
first words to Elvis Presley,
1955**

My voice alone is just an ordinary voice. What people come to see is how I use it. If I stand still while I'm singing… I'm dead. I might as well go back to driving a truck. **,,**

1956

"

Your legs have been shaking with the music and your eyes twitching and your shoulders twitching and everything! Get out there and keep doing it!

"

**Colonel Tom Parker,
1956**

More than anything else, I want the folks back at home to think right of me.

1956

"

I'd just like to be treated like a regular customer.

1956

"

I hope I didn't bore you too much with my life story.

1957

I like to sing ballads the way Eddie Fisher does and the way Perry Como does. But the way I'm singing now is what makes the money.

1956

I happened to come along in the music business when there was no trend.

1955

"

File your application at the door, honey.

Elvis, when asked "Are you planning on taking any more gals to Memphis?", 1957

"

"

Honey, I prefer to date 'em all until I find the right one.

"

**Elvis, when asked about a current
"Number One girlfriend",
1957**

"

My movements, ma'am, are all leg movements. I don't do nothing with my body.

1956

"

Those people in New York are not gonna change me none. I'm gonna show you what the real Elvis is like tonight.

1956

"

You know what they want – dirt.
But I'm not a dirt farmer.

,,

Colonel Tom Parker
on writing his own book on Elvis,
1977

The closest I ever came to getting married was just before I started singing. In fact, my first record saved my neck.

1956

The Army can do anything it wants
with me.

1958

Well, he's got a good voice, good singer, if we can find the right material. **"**

Scotty Moore, about Elvis, 1956

"

It's not how much you have that makes people look up to you, it's who you are.

"

I am not in love now. But I can't
guarantee about tomorrow.

**Elvis, when asked if he was in love,
1957**

"

I never sang like that in my life, until I made that first record… I remembered that song because I heard Arthur [Crudup] sing it, and I thought I would like to try it. That was it.

"

Elvis, on "That's All Right",
his first recording,
1954

That's not true at all. Elvis takes fifty per cent of everything I earn." Colonel Tom Parker, when asked by a reporter, "Is it true that you take fifty per cent of everything Elvis earns?

1968

"

Elvis didn't die, the body did. We're keeping Elvis alive. I talked to him this morning and he told me to carry on.

"

**Colonel Tom Parker's first words
to the media, after news of Elvis's death
broke around the world,
1977**

It was getting harder and harder to sing to a camera all day.

1969,
Elvis's response when asked
why he returned to live performing

"

One of these days, I'll probably fall apart. I feel, I've just been lucky.

Elvis, when asked by a reporter on
how he manages to stay looking
so young,
1969

When you do 10 songs in a movie,
they can't all be good songs. "

1969

"

I got tired of singing to turtles.

Elvis, on his movie career,
1969

I don't favour any one type.
I like girls!

**Elvis, when asked about his preferences,
1957**

❝

It's not secluded, honey. I'm just sneaky.

❞

**Elvis, when asked by a reporter,
"Why have you led such a secluded
life all these years?",
1969**

Ambition is a dream with a V8 engine.

"

CHAPTER

TWO

TAKING CARE
OF BUSINESS

"

Values are like fingerprints. Nobody's are the same, but you leave 'em all over everything you do.

"

It's all a big hoax, honey. I never wrote a song in my life. I get one-third of the credit for recording it. It makes me look smarter than I am. I've never even had an idea for a song. Just once, maybe. **"**

1957

"

After a hard day of basic training,
you could eat a rattlesnake.

"

Heck, no. Colonel Parker only advises me on business matters and that's all! I'm young, have to do what I want. I hardly ever see him.

Elvis, when asked if Colonel Tom Parker rules his private life, 1957

I went to bed one night, had quite a dream, and woke up all shook up. I phoned a pal and told him about it. By morning, he had a new song, 'All Shook Up'.

1957

People ask me where I got my singing style. I didn't copy my style from anybody.

Truth is like the sun. You can shut it out for a time, but it ain't goin' away.

Rock-'n'-roll music, if you like it, if you feel it, you can't help but move to it. That's what happens to me. I can't help it.

Some people tap their feet, some people snap their fingers, and some people sway back and forth. I just sorta do 'em all together, I guess.

1956

'Jailhouse Rock'. It's the hardest song to sing that I've ever recorded. My tongue practically falls out on this one.

1957

When things go wrong, don't go with them.

"

I'd like to say that I learned very early in life that 'Without a song, the day would never end; without a song, a man ain't got a friend; without a song, the road would never bend – without a song.' So I keep singing a song.

1970

"

I have no use for bodyguards, but I have very specific use for two highly trained certified public accountants.

"

I'm just like a robot getting in and out. I just follow along, that's all. I leave before the audience knows I'm out of the building. They tell me to be at a certain door by 10.10 p.m. and I am! No bows, no curtain calls. I finish the last number, and away I go.

1957

The image is one thing and the human being is another. It's very hard to live up to an image, put it that way.

1972

"

The Lord can give, and the Lord can take away. I might be herding sheep next year.

1956

"

Sad thing is, you can still love someone and be wrong for them.

I sure lost my musical direction in Hollywood. My songs were the same conveyor-belt mass production, just like most of my movies were.

"

'Old Shep' was the first song I ever did in life; I won $5 in a contest singin' it.

"

1957

No, I see no point in studying. I don't think I need it, do you? But there is one thing, I'd like to be a good actor. I'm always striving to be natural in front of the camera. That takes studying, of a sort.

1957

"

I was an only child, and Mother was always right with me all my life. I used to get very angry at her when I was growing up — it's a natural thing.

"

To judge a man by his weakest link or deed is like judging the power of the ocean by one wave.

Rock 'n' roll is a music, and why should a music contribute to… juvenile delinquency? If people are going to be juvenile delinquents, they're going to be delinquents if they hear… Mother Goose rhymes.

1956

I'm never going to sing another song I don't believe in. I'm never going to make another picture I don't believe in.

1968

It just happened. I like to sing, and, well, I just started singing and folks just started listening. I can't tell folks that I worked and learned and studied, and overcame disappointments, because I didn't.

1968

When I was a child, I was a dreamer. I read comic books, and I was the hero of the comic book. I saw movies, and I was the hero in the movie. So every dream I ever dreamed, has come true a hundred times.

1971

The first time that I appeared on stage, it scared me to death. I really didn't know what all the yelling was about. I didn't realize that my body was moving. It's a natural thing to me. So to the manager backstage I said, 'What'd I do? What'd I do?' And he said, 'Whatever it is, go back and do it again.'

1972

A live concert to me is exciting because of all the electricity that is generated in the crowd and on stage. It's my favourite part of the business – live concerts. 🔑🔑

1973

"

A lot of people have accused Elvis of stealing the black man's music, when, in fact, almost every black solo entertainer copied his stage mannerisms from Elvis.

Jackie Wilson

"

"

Elvis is the greatest cultural force in the twentieth century. He introduced the beat to everything, music, language, clothes, it's a whole new social revolution – the '60s comes from it.

**Leonard Bernstein,
1977**

"

THREE

MAKE YOUR

MAMA PROUD

"

When I first heard Elvis's voice I just knew that I wasn't going to work for anybody; and nobody was going to be my boss… Hearing him for the first time was like busting out of jail.

Bob Dylan

"

Before Elvis, there was nothing.

John Lennon

Rock-and-roll music, if you like it, if you feel it, you can't help but move to it. That's what happens to me. I can't help it.

1956

I wouldn't knock Frank Sinatra. I like him very much. If I remember correctly, he was also part of a trend, just like rock 'n' roll. I think it's the greatest music ever naturally 'cause it's the only thing I can do! If I were a pop singer, I'd prefer pop,

1957

Who am I to sit here and knock someone else? If someone has strived for something, then it's OK. I don't dig in and question it. I never knock anyone who's successful.

1957

You can't stay on top forever. Even if I stopped singing tomorrow, I'd have no regrets. I had a ball while I was there.

1957

"

I don't know exactly how much I've made. It's over a million a year.

1957

I wish you'd straighten out somethin' right here. Many magazines have printed that I have eight Gold Records, but I believe in giving a man credit for what he's done, and I've had 19 Gold Records!

Don't criticize what you don't understand, son. You never walked in that man's shoes.

1955

I don't like to be called Elvis the Pelvis. It's one of the most childish expressions I've ever heard coming from an adult. But if they wanna call me that, there's nothin' I can do about it, so I just have to accept it. Just like you gotta accept the good with the bad, the bad with the good.

When I started singing, I weighed 153 pounds. I weigh 184 now. I haven't gotten any taller, but I'm putting on a little more weight.

Any audience, as a rule, goes for a
fast number.

99

"

I like pork chops and country ham, creamed potatoes, stuff like that. Redeye gravy. It comes from ham, bacon, stuff like that. It's the grease that you fry it in. I eat a lot of Jell-O. Fruit Jell-O.

"

In public, I like real conservative clothes, something that's not too flashy. But onstage, I like 'em as flashy as you can get 'em.

I went into Sun Records and there was a guy in there took down my name, told me he might call me sometime. So he called me about a year and a half later, and I went in and made my first record, 'That's All Right, Mama'.

"

I watch my audience and listen to 'em, and I know that we're all getting somethin' out of our system. None of us knows what it is. The important thing is we're getting rid of it and nobody's getting hurt.

The first car I bought was the most beautiful car I've ever seen. It was second-hand, but I parked it outside of my hotel the day I got it. I sat up all night, just lookin' at it.

You have to put on a show for people in order to draw a crowd. If I just stood out there and sang and didn't move a muscle, then people would say, 'My goodness, I can stay home and listen to his records.' You have to give them a show.

"
I hate to turn anybody down who wants an autograph. **"**

My mother never really wanted anything fancy. She just stayed the same all the way through the whole thing. I wish — there's a lot of things happened since she passed away that would've made her very happy and very proud. But that's life.

I've had a pretty good lesson in human nature. It's more important to try to surround yourself with people who can give you a little happiness, because you only pass through this life once, Jack. You don't come back for an encore.

The hardest part of the entire military service; is being away from the fans and just being away from show business all year. That was the hardest part of all. It wasn't the Army, it wasn't the other men, it was that. It stayed on my mind. I kept thinking about the past all the time, contemplating the future and that was the hardest part.

"

They don't bother me… I wish
them luck.

Elvis, on the Beatles
1964

"

I'll admit something to you. But without going into details. Let me say that I've led quite a fast life, really, and that I'm as red-blooded as the next guy.

1964

"

This is not the way the Colonel sees it. And I trust the Colonel.

"

Elvis, when asked why he had not performed live outside the United States, 1964

Remember, I am a lucky guy myself.
I've never forgotten that. It's too
vivid in my memory. I'll say that
the Beatles have got what it takes,
and in great abundance, that they
have been given a heck of a vote
of confidence.

1964

I am most grateful for my good fortune. But I am a man of simple tastes. I don't need the money for myself. For a while, I was like a kid with a new toy, but it was never my goal and never will be. **"**

1964

Money can never buy everything your heart desires. It won't buy love, or health or true happiness. And even sometimes when you give it away, you don't get the thanks you're entitled to.

1964

CHAPTER

FOUR

ALL SHOOK UP

"

I have left it to the Colonel to guide my career and I trust him because he knows his business like nobody else. But I draw my own conclusions and make my own decisions... which includes anything from picking the songs for my new film, to cutting a new record, to falling in love. **"**

**Elvis, when asked how much
Colonel Tom Parker is the boss,
1964**

The sideburns did it, I think.

Elvis, when asked how he became successful in rock 'n' roll without long hair, 1965

I was raised, you know, in a pretty decent home and everything. My folks always made me behave, whether I wanted to or not. **"**

1956

I don't see that any type of music would have any bad influence on people, it's only music. I mean, I can't figure it out. I mean in a lot of the papers they say that rock 'n' roll is a bad influence – I don't think it is.

1956

❝

How would rock-'n'-roll music make anybody rebel against their parents?

❞

1956

You know, one of the things reporters write about me is that I try to do everything perfect. Maybe I try too hard sometimes. But they're right. I feel I've got to do my best, whatever I try.

1956

I sing the way I do, and act the way I do, because it comes naturally to me while I'm singing. I wouldn't do it if I thought it wasn't the right thing to do, or if I thought someone was being hurt by it. If I thought that, I'd pack up and go back home and never sing another note.

1956

If I stood up in front of an audience and did nothing but sing, I'd be holding myself back deliberate. I wouldn't enjoy myself, I couldn't enjoy myself if I did that. And the audience would know it. They'd know I didn't enjoy what I was doing, and they wouldn't come out to see me again the next time.

1956

One of the things [reporters] said about me is that I'm never nervous. They say I don't worry about a thing and they say I get eight or ten good hours sleep at night. I wish they were right.

1956

I've never had a singing lesson in my life. No music lesson of any kind, in fact. I just started singing when I was a little kid and I've been doing it ever since.

1956

When I was 13 or so, me and a bunch of the kids would fool around singing. I sure enjoyed beating up a storm with the other kids. And you know how it is. You get to trying different ways of using your voice and singing the words and such, and pretty soon you're singing in a style of your own.

"

I got my practice in singing by just experimenting around and singing with the other kids at school and having a good time. And most important, singing the way I felt. And to tell you the truth, I think it's the best kind of practice I could have had.

"

All of my life, I've wanted to be an actor, though I never was in any school plays or recited a line other than the Gettysburg Address for my sixth-grade homeroom class. But always sticking in the back of my head was the idea that, somehow, someday, I'd like to get the chance to act.

"

I came out to Hollywood almost three months ago, and Mr Hal Wallis of Paramount Pictures asked me to take a screen test. He told me to just act like myself. I studied up on what they wanted me to do, and then before I knew it I was in front of the camera.

I wonder if you can ever know what it's like to be standing in a movie sound stage and hear a bell ring and people shout, 'Quiet!', and then all of a sudden realize that everyone's watching you, and you're supposed to be acting out a part. I'll tell you, it's enough to make your legs slide out from under you.

99

I've heard so many stories about why I grew my sideburns that I just can't help from laughing sometimes… because there wasn't a lick of truth to the things they said.

"

66

I believe all good things come from God.

" When I was driving a pick-up truck in Memphis, I used to dream about being a success and wondered how my life would change if it should ever happen. Well, I can tell you how I feel about it now. I don't feel a bit different now than I did before all this happened. I'm just like I always was. "

"

I just wish, that everybody could know the same kind of happiness I've known from all my success. I wish that, more than anything, with all my heart.

"

I just finished my first movie for 20th Century Fox, called *Love Me Tender*, and you know, it was the biggest thrill of my life. I'd sure like to keep on making pictures for you.

"

I can plunk on it pretty good, and follow a tune if I'm really pressed to do it. But I've never won any prizes and I never will.

"

**Elvis, when asked if he can
actually play the guitar,
1956**

My mouth waters every time I think of momma's bacon-and-egg breakfast. I sure fill up on 'em when I'm home!

Everybody asks me: why do I sing like I do? I know as well as you what some people are saying. I'm not deaf. I can hear it same as you. They don't like dancing. They don't like western music. They don't like rock 'n' roll. And they don't like me.

My momma taught me one thing right from the very beginning, and that's that everyone's got a right to his own opinion. I believe that. And I also believe that you can't make everyone like you, no matter who you are.

I can't explain what happens when the music starts. But I think I know. I think you know what it is to get all tied up in something, to get lost in it. That's what singing and music does to me. It ties me up. It makes me forget everything else except the beat and the sound. It tells me more than anything else I've ever known, how good, how great it is just to be alive.

99

I've been singing the way I do now as far back as I can remember. I don't know what style you'd call it or anything like that. All I know is I sing the way I do because it comes to me natural.

99

A lot of people ask me, 'Are you trying to copy somebody, the way you sing?' All I can tell 'em is what I honestly know in my heart. I've never tried to copy anybody.

When I was called to make my first record, I went to the studio and they told me what they wanted me to sing and how they wanted me to sing it. Well, I tried it their way, but it didn't work out so good.

“

Mr (Sam) Phillips, the man who owned the recording company, said I should go ahead and sing all the songs my own way, the way I knew best.

”

When Mr Phillips called me to make that first record, I went into the studio and started singing. I started jumping up and down, they tell me, and I wasn't even aware of it. My legs were shaking all over, mostly because I was so nervous and excited, but also because I can feel the music more when I just let myself react.

99

CHAPTER

FIVE

NOTHING BUT A
HOUND DOG

If rock-'n'-roll music were to die out – which I don't think it will – I would try something else. I would really probably go in for the movies then and I would try to make it as an actor, which is very tough because you got a lot of competition. **"**

1957

It's like a guy down in Fort Hood…
one of the sergeants one day…
I was… I was sitting down on my
foot locker and my left leg was
shaking. I mean just unconsciously.
He said, 'Presley, I wish you'd quit
shaking that leg.' I said, 'Sarge, when
that leg quits shaking, I'm finished.'

1957

When I got out of high school I was driving a truck. I was just a poor boy from Memphis. I was driving a truck and training to be an electrician. I suppose I got wired the wrong way round somewhere along the line.

Would I like to spend more time in the Army? Like I said, I was anxious to get back to show business. I'll answer that by saying I'm glad I served the two years and that it worked out as well as it did, but I'm very happy to get back into what I was doing.

1960

"

I'm gonna sing and I'll let the shaking come naturally. If I had to stand still and sing I'd be lost. I can't get any feeling that way.

"

1960

I made four movies and, in 1958, I got drafted… I went into the Army and stayed a couple of years. That was loads-a-fun… They made a big deal outta cuttin' all my hair off and all that jazz. I was a soldier, now. The next thing I knew, I was out of the service and making movies, again. My first picture was called *GI Blues* and I thought I was still in the army!

"

"

I did some good pictures that did very well for me, like *Blue Hawaii*… and some pretty forgettable ones, too!

"

I love the live contact with an audience. It was getting harder and harder to perform to a movie camera all day long. The inspiration wasn't there. I'm tired of playing a guy singing to the guy he's beating up.

1969

For the first three songs or so, before I loosened up. Then I thought, 'What the heck. Get with it, man, or you might be out of a job tomorrow.'

Elvis, when asked if he was nervous about returning to singing live, 1969

"

Well, I'd like to make better films.

"

**Elvis, when asked what type
of films he'd like to make,
1970**

All kidding aside, it happened very fast to all of us, my mother and my father and all of us. And everything happened overnight, and so we had to adjust to a lot of things very quickly… I don't really miss that much about it. I enjoy it just as much now or more than I did then. I would like to think that we've improved ourselves over the past fifteen years.

1972

Rhythm is something you either have or don't have, but when you have it, you have it all over.

"

"

I'm in too far to get out.

The more happiness money helps to create, the more it's worth. It's worthless as an old cut-up paper if it just lays in a bank and grows there without ever having been used to help a body.

1968

I've tried to lead a straight, clean life, not set any kind of a bad example.

I'm not trying to be sexy. It's just my way of expressing myself when I move around.

A Presley picture is the only sure thing in Hollywood.

Hal Wallis

Mother, I would give every dime I have and even dig ditches just to have you back.

Elvis's final words to his mother,
Gladys, at her funeral,
1958

"

I don't know why she had to go so young. But it made me think about death. I don't feel I'll live a long life. That's why I have to get what I can from every day.

"

Elvis, about the death of his mother, Gladys, 1958

I don't sound like nobody.

**Elvis to Sun Records receptionist
Marion Kessler, the first time he entered Sun
Studios, when asked, "So, who do you sound like?"
1953**

"

She's all I ever lived for. She was always my best girl. **"**

Elvis, about his mother, Gladys
1958

I'm still afraid to this day that one morning I'll wake up and find out that everything was a dream and that we're all still back in Tupelo with no hope of getting out from under the poverty.

1970

You can't go on doing the same thing year after year. It's been a long time since I've done anything professional, except make movies and cut albums… Before long, I'm going to make some personal-appearance tours… I want to see some places I've never seen before. I miss the personal contact with audiences.

1968

I never felt poor. There was always shoes to wear and food to eat – yet I knew there were things my parents did without just to make sure I was clothed and fed.

"

My next move was to Hollywood. That's how it works. You get a record and then you get on television and then they take you to Hollywood to make a picture. So I did *Love Me Tender*, then I did *Loving You*. I wasn't ready for that town and they weren't ready for me.

"

1956

It's true, I do have four Cadillacs. I haven't got any use for four. Maybe some day, I'll go broke and I can sell a couple of 'em.

“

Man, I really like Vegas.

Priscilla is going to have a baby…
We're going to have another
rock-'n'-roll singer!

SIX

ELVIS HAS LEFT THE BUILDING

"

Why buy a cow when you can get milk through the fence?

"

Elvis, when asked if he would marry, 1956

I lose myself in my singing. Maybe it's my early training singing gospel hymns. I'm limp as a rag, worn out, when a show's over.

1957

My fans want my shirt. They can have my shirt. They put it on my back.

1957

"

It's the greatest ever, mainly because
it's all I can do.

"

**Elvis, when asked "What do you think
of rock 'n' roll?",
1957**

"

I just know that, right now… the biggest record-selling business there is… is rock 'n' roll.

1956

"

The trouble is, when a fellow is by himself and starts thinking, the sad things are always stronger in his memory than the happy things.

1968

"

I don't regard money or position as important. But I can never forget the longing to be someone. I guess if you are poor, you always think bigger and want more than those who have everything when they are born.

"

1965

Is it another of those Highness deals?

**Elvis, when preparing to meet
a group of Scandanavian princesses,
1960**

My daddy knew a lot of guitar players, and most of them didn't work, so he said, 'You should make your mind up to either be a guitar player or an electrician, but I never saw a guitar player that was worth a damn.'

1972

Well, sir, it's very hard to live up to an image.
"

Since I was two years old, all I knew was gospel music. That music became such a part of my life, it was as natural as dancing. A way to escape from the problems. And my way of release.

1977

"

Clothes say things about you that you can't, sometimes.

"

My mother and dad both loved to sing. They tell me when I was about three or four years old, I got away from them in church and walked up in the front of the choir and started beating time.

"

I had seen him go by in his Crown Electric truck a number of different times, because we had an open storefront. He would go by and go back – and go by and go back. This guy would not come in the studio and ask me to audition him for nothing.

Sam Phillips

"

It shocked me because here was a classic blues number and here was a white cat not imitating or mimicking but just putting his feel into it. It blew me away.

"

Sam Phillips, when Elvis delivered an impromptu uptempo performance of Arthur Crudup's blues number "That's All Right", 1954 – a breakthrough moment.

Everybody thinks Sam was looking for a white boy to do black music, but Elvis was looking for Sam Phillips.

Jerry Schilling

"

'Oh, what do we have here?'

"

Elvis, on first seeing Priscilla Beaulieu, 1967

The humdrum movies he was given – boy chases girl, boy gets girl, they get married and it's happily ever after – that was not Elvis Presley. He was not that man. He was much deeper than that. After a movie, he felt trapped. He dreaded the next script because he knew it would be the same thing over and over again.

Priscilla Presley

" Man, I just work here! **"**

**Elvis, when he told the fans
he was leaving the stage**

I take vitamin E! No, I was only kidding. I just… embarrassed myself, man. I don't know, dear. I just enjoy the business. I like what I'm doing." Elvis, when asked why he thinks he has outlasted every other entertainer.

1972

I wanted to say to Elvis Presley and the country that this is a real decent, fine boy.

**Ed Sullivan,
1957**

Oh, I don't know what makes them think that, I got, you know, this gold belt.

Elvis, when told people think he is a wonderful, shy and humble human being, 1972

"

It was the finest music of his life. If ever there was music that bleeds, this was it.

"

Greil Marcus, on Elvis's legendary comeback 1968 TV Special

I ride horseback, swim and talk with
the tourists hanging out at the gates.

Elvis, on what he gets up to
at Graceland,
1969

I don't think I'm bad for people. If I did think I was bad for people, I would go back to driving a truck, and I really mean this.

1956

"

Honey, I'd just sooner keep my own personal views about that to myself 'cause I'm just an entertainer and I'd rather not say.

Elvis, when asked about Vietnam War protesters,
1972

"

The press makes entertainers, and the deejays, too. If the press didn't write, no one would know what you're doing. Everyone needs the press.

"

1957

I think I have something tonight that's not quite correct for evening wear: blue suede shoes.

1956

"

How I got in this business and how I got started, where and when, and so forth... it's been written up so many times, people don't even know the true story.

"

1969